JUST THE FACTS

A Short and Concise Guide to
My Life, Estate, and Wishes

· ·

NAME AND DATE

CONFIDENTIAL

This portfolio contains confidential information
and should be stored in a safe place.

Published by 55 Plus Essential Services, LLC
www.55PlusES.com
Copyright © 2023 Susan Loumagne

Author: Susan Loumagne

Graphic Support: Lawrence Phillips

ISBN: 979-8-9867618-8-6

This book is not a legal document nor is it a Will.
No liability is assumed for losses or damages due to the information provided.

TABLE OF CONTENTS

Welcome Page 5

Quick Start Guide 6

Resources 7

Useful listings for replacement of important documents, government resources, and getting a Will and Healthcare Directives.

To-Do Notes 8

Use these pages to track what you need to do, find, or replace

Personal Profile and Important Contacts 9

Parents, siblings, children, employment, volunteerism, military service, and storage of important papers

Pet Information 15

Name, type of pet, veterinarian, medications, vaccines, microchip status, pet insurance, notable markings, health conditions, and your pet care service.

Finances 18

Banking, credit cards, personal income, financial advisor and investments, insurance policies – life, property, auto, health, dental, and tax records

Assets 28

Storage of keys, garage door code, hidden assets, real estate, vehicles, loans given, and personal property

Estate and Legal Documents 34

Will, executor, power of attorney, and healthcare directives

Medical and Medications.. 36

Doctors, medical conditions, and medications

Final Wishes... 39

Designation of your final disposition, funeral home, viewing, obituary, graveside, military honors, service, and reception

Passwords 42

Cell phone, computer, websites, and social media,

Monthly Bills, Subscriptions, and Giving 44

Record your obligations for household bills and recurring payments

Thoughts, Words, and Wishes.. 47

Words you live by, thoughts, and your wishes for the future.

If I'm Unable to Communicate... 48

A list of what to do and who to contact.

Additional Information... 49
Open space to share anything not covered in any section.

Memorable Moments.. 50

Letters to Loved Ones (*pages for two letters*) 51

WELCOME

The Just the Facts Guide is easy to use and ensures you capture the most important information about your estate and wishes. In the event of unexpected illness, incapacity, or passing, your loved ones will appreciate having this vital information.

When filling out this guide, we encourage you to revisit past decisions about your Will, insurance, and other coverages and make updates to ensure their relevance. If you do not have a Will or Healthcare Directive, take the time now and create them. The Resources Page includes a few options for you to consider.

Be sure to inform your loved ones that you have this guide and where it is stored. In addition, we suggest discussing your wishes and designations with your loved ones or attorney to ensure clarity and understanding.

We recommend the following:

- ✓ *Complete only the sections and information that apply to you.*
- ✓ *Use the "To Do Notes" to track what you need to do, find, or replace.*
- ✓ *The Just The Facts Guide is also available in a digital version. Email kindleforms@55pluses.com*
- ✓ *We value your feedback and would appreciate it if you would leave a review on Amazon with your thoughts about the Just the Facts Guide.*

This planner is not a legal document and cannot be considered a Will or any other legal document.

QUICK START GUIDE TO COMPLETING YOUR PERSONAL AFFAIRS PORTFOLIO

The following tips will help ensure that you complete your Guide.

1: Schedule It

Block off time this week to begin your Guide. At the end of the session, schedule the next time you will work on the next sections.

2: Do It

You may want to work with a partner. One person writes while the other dictates the information. Only fill in the information you feel comfortable adding. For example, you may want to use only the last 4 digits of your Social Security number or credit card account.

3: To-Do List

Use the To-Do page to keep a list of what information and documents you need to find, copy, or replace.

4: Photo and Video It

Take photos of your family and pets for identification purposes. In addition, take photos and videos of your home's contents and exterior, so you'll have a visual record for yourself and insurance claims.

5. Follow Up

Order copies of missing documents and complete all lingering tasks on your list. The Resource Page has links to help you obtain originals of any essential missing cards or documents.

6: Store It

We recommend storing this Guide with your essential legal and estate documents, photos, letters to loved ones, and other necessary and important items you've referenced. It's wise to purchase a fireproof and waterproof lock box with a one-hour (minimum) fireproof rating to store these items.

7: Share It

Let trusted people know that you have this Guide and where it is stored. It is also the perfect time to initiate hard-to-have conversations to discuss your estate and let people know your wishes.

RESOURCES

Vital Records

Birth, Death, Marriage, and Divorce Records　　　　www.cdc.gov/nchs/w2w.htm

Link to your state's Bureau of Vital Statistics

Government Programs

Medicare　　　　　　　　　　　　　　　　www.medicare.gov
800-633-4227

Social Security Office　　　　　　　　　　www.socialsecurity.gov
800-772-1213

Veterans Administration　　　　　　　　　www.va.gov
800-827-1000

Veterans Service Records National Archives　　www.archives.gov/veterans
866-272-6272

Passports – U.S. Passports　　　　　　　　www.travel.state.gov
877-487-2778

Estate and Must Have Documents

Wills, Healthcare Directives, and Durable Power of Attorney

National Academy of Elder Law Attorneys　　www.naela.org
703-942-5711

Legal Zoom　　　　　　　　　　　　　　www.legalzoom.com
800-773-0888

Emergency Preparation & Disaster Relief

American Red Cross　　　　　　　　　　　www.redcross.org
800-733-2767

FEMA – Federal Emergency Management Association　www.fema.gov
800-621-3362

Ready.gov　　　　　　　　　　　　　　　www.ready.gov
800-621-3362

TO DO NOTES

....
....
....
....
....
....
....
....
....
....
....
....
....
....
....
....
....
....
....
....
....
....

PERSONAL PROFILE

Name: ....

Birth Date: .... Place of Birth: ....

Name on Birth Certificate: ....

Mother's Maiden Name: .... Living? ....

....

Father's Name: .... Living? ....

....

Relationship Status: .... Spouse/Partner's Name: ....

....

Employed By: ....

Job Title: ....

Supervisor's Name and Phone Number: ....

....

Volunteer Organizations and Contact:..

....

....

Military Branch: .... Rank: ....:......................

Dates Served and Where? ....

....

NOTES ....

....

....

....

IMPORTANT PAPERS

Examples of important papers are social security card, birth certificate, passport, driver's license, military DD214, marriage license, divorce record, resident alien card, adoption record, frequent traveler #.

Type	Number	Stored Where?	Copy Y/N

SIBLINGS

Name: .... Birth Date: ....

Phone: .... Living?: ....

Email or Address:.......... ....

Name: .... Birth Date: ....

Phone: .... Living?: ....

Email or Address: ....

Name: .... Birth Date: ....

Phone: .... Living?: ....

Email or Address: ....

Name: .... Birth Date: ....

Phone: .... Living?: ....

Email or Address: ....

Name: .... Birth Date: ....

Phone: .... Living?: ....

Email or Address: ....

Name: .... Birth Date: ....

Phone: .... Living?: ....

Email or Address: ....

CHILDREN

Name of Parents: ....

Social Security Number Optional

Given Name: ....

Date of Birth: .... Place of Birth: ....

SS#: .... Phone Number: ....

Email: ....

Given Name: ....

Date of Birth: .... Place of Birth: ....

SS#: .... Phone Number: ....

Email: ....

Given Name: ....

Date of Birth: .... Place of Birth: ....

SS#: .... Phone Number: ....

Email: ....

Given Name: ....

Date of Birth: .... Place of Birth: ....

SS#: .... Phone Number: ....

Email: ....

Given Name: ....

Date of Birth: .... Place of Birth: ....

SS#: .... Phone Number: ....

Email: ....

IMPORTANT CONTACTS

Name: .... Relationship: ....

Phone: .... Phone: ....

Email or Address: ....

Name: .... Relationship: ....

Phone: .... Phone: ....

Email or Address: ....

Name: .... Relationship: ....

Phone: ....Phone: ....

Email or Address: ....

Name: .... Relationship: ....

Phone: .... Phone: ....

Email or Address: ....

Name: .... Relationship: ....

Phone: .... Phone: ....

Email or Address: ....

Name: .... Relationship: ....

Phone: .... Phone: ....

Email or Address: ....

IMPORTANT CONTACTS

Name: .... Relationship: ....

Phone: .... Phone: ....

Email or Address: ....

Name: .... Relationship: ....

Phone: .... Phone: ....

Email or Address: ....

Name: .... Relationship: ....

Phone: .... Phone: ....

Email or Address: ....

Name: .... Relationship: ....

Phone: .... Phone: ....

Email or Address: ....

Name: .... Relationship: ....

Phone: .... Phone: ....

Email or Address: ....

Name: .... Relationship: ....

Phone: .... Phone: ....

Email or Address: ....

PET INFORMATION

Pet Name: .... Date of Birth: .... Age: ....

Breed: .... Coat Color: ....

☐ Canine/Dog ☐ Feline/Cat ☐ Neutered or Spayed Other: ....

Notable markings on pet: ....

Veterinarian name and phone number: ....

....

24-hour Veterinarian name and phone number: ....

....

Is this a service animal with certification? ....

Where do you keep the certification document? ....

Any Medical or Behavioral Alerts? Seizures, caution with humans or other animals, adverse reactions to medications, allergies, blind, or deaf. ....

....

....

IDENTIFICATION

Does your pet have identification tags with your name and phone number? Y/N
What name and number are on the tags? ....

....

Does your pet have a microchip or tattoo? ....

....

What is the number? ....

....

Local shelter name and phone number: ....

....

Local shelter name and phone number: ....

....

VACCINES

Common Vaccines: Bordetella, Lepto, DHPP, DHLPP, Rattlesnake, FVRCP, Feline Leukemia

Date of Last Rabies Vaccine: ....

Name of Vaccine: .... Date: ....

Name of Vaccine: .... Date: ....

Name of Vaccine: .... Date: ....

Name of Vaccine: .... Date: ....

Name of Vaccine: .... Date: ....

Name of Vaccine: .... Date: ....

MEDICATIONS

Is your pet on medications? ....

Name of medications: ....

....

Where do you purchase the medications? ....

....

If online, what is the website and account information?...

....

Account User ID: .... Password: ....

Are your orders on auto-delivery? ....

....

Additional notes: ....

....

INSURANCE

Do you have pet insurance? ....

....

What is the company name and policy number? ....

....

....

PET CARE SERVICE

List the name of the people or companies you use for pet care: walking, feeding, or overnights.

Name: .... Phone Number: ....

Name: .... Phone Number: ....

LONG-TERM CARE PLANNING

Have you designated someone to care for your pet if you are unable? ....

Name and contact information: ....

....

Details of the arrangement: ....

....

....

....

Have you done estate planning for your pet and included it as part of your Will? ....

Details of the arrangement: ....

....

....

....

Additional notes about your pet: ....

....

FINANCES

BANKING *Add log-in information to Password Section*

Name of Bank: ....

Branch Location: ....

Contact's Name: .... Phone No: ....

Account Type	Account Number * optional	Name on Account

Notes: ....

Name of Bank: ....

Branch Location: ....

Contact's Name: .... Phone No: ....

Account Type	Account Number * optional	Name on Account

Notes: ....

Name of Bank: ....

Branch Location: ....

Contact's Name: .... Phone No: ....

Account Type	Account Number * optional	Name on Account

Notes: ....

CREDIT CARDS

* Account number and security code optional.   *Add log-in information to the Passwords Section.*

Name of Company: .... Phone No: ....

Name on Account: ....

Account Number: .... Security Code: ....

Expiration: .... Balance Insured: ....

Name of Company: .... Phone No: ....

Name on Account: ....

Account Number: .... Security Code: ....

Expiration: .... Balance Insured: ....

Name of Company: .... Phone No: ....

Name on Account: ....

Account Number: .... Security Code: ....

Expiration: .... Balance Insured: ....

Name of Company: .... Phone No: ....

Name on Account: ....

Account Number: .... Security Code: ....

Expiration: .... Balance Insured: ....

Name of Company: .... Phone No: ....

Name on Account: ....

Account Number: .... Security Code: ....

Expiration: .... Balance Insured: ....

FINANCIAL SERVICES and CD'S

Financial Services Company: ....

Advisor's Name: .... Phone Number: ....

Address: ....

Notes: ....

....

Advisor's Name: .... Phone Number: ....

Address: ....

Notes: ....

....

CERTIFICATE OF DEPOSIT

Bank: ....

Amount: .... Interest Rate: .... Maturity Date: ....

Bank: ....

Amount: .... Interest Rate: .... Maturity Date: ....

Bank: ....

Amount: .... Interest Rate: .... Maturity Date: ....

Bank: ....

Amount: .... Interest Rate: .... Maturity Date: ....

SAVINGS BONDS STORAGE

....

....

....

INVESTMENTS

Investment Type: .... * 401K, IRA, Mutual Funds, Stocks, Bitcoin, NFT's

Held By: .... Phone Number: ....

Account Number: ....

Notes:..

....

Investment Type: .... * 401K, IRA, Mutual Funds, Stocks, Bitcoin, NFT's

Held By: .... Phone Number: ....

Account Number: ....

Notes:..

....

Investment Type: .... * 401K, IRA, Mutual Funds, Stocks, Bitcoin, NFT's

Held By: .... Phone Number: ....

Account Number: ....

Notes:..

....

Investment Type: .... * 401K, IRA, Mutual Funds, Stocks, Bitcoin, NFT's

Held By: .... Phone Number: ....

Account Number: ....

Notes:..

....

Investment Type: .... * 401K, IRA, Mutual Funds, Stocks, Bitcoin, NFT's

Held By: .... Phone Number: ....

Account Number: ....

Notes:..

....

PERSONAL INCOME

This section covers any income you receive; salary, social security, pensions, annuities, military, trusts, royalties, bonuses, dividends, interest, alimony, or any other income you receive.

Type:* ....

Company: .... Phone: ....

Amount: .... Note: ....

Type:* ....

Company: .... Phone: ....

Amount: .... Note: ....

Type:* ....

Company: .... Phone: ....

Amount: .... Note: ....

Type:* ....

Company: .... Phone: ....

Amount: .... Note: ....

Type:* ....

Company: .... Phone: ....

Amount: .... Note: ....

Type:* ....

Company: .... Phone: ....

Amount: .... Note: ....

Type:* ....

Company: .... Phone: ....

Amount: .... Note: ....

LOANS YOU OWE

Loan From: .... Phone: ....

Account Number: ....

Type of Loan: .... Interest Rate: ....

Amount: .... Payment: ....

Date of Origination: .... Length of Loan: ....

Loan From: .... Phone: ....

Account Number: ....

Type of Loan: .... Interest Rate: ....

Amount: .... Payment: ....

Date of Origination: .... Length of Loan: ....

Loan From: .... Phone: ....

Account Number: ....

Type of Loan: .... Interest Rate: ....

Amount: .... Payment: ....

Date of Origination: .... Length of Loan: ....

Loan From: .... Phone: ....

Account Number: ....

Type of Loan: .... Interest Rate: ....

Amount: .... Payment: ....

Date of Origination: .... Length of Loan: ....

Loan From: .... Phone: ....

Account Number: ....

Type of Loan: .... Interest Rate: ....

Amount: .... Payment: ....

Date of Origination: .... Length of Loan: ....

INSURANCE

AUTO INSURANCE - vehicle make, model, Vin# are also in the Assets section.

Company: .... Phone: ....

Policy Number: .... Policy Stored Where? ....

Agent Name: .... Agent Phone: ....

Company: .... Phone: ....

Policy Number: .... Policy Stored Where? ....

Agent Name: .... Agent Phone: ....

HEALTH, DENTAL, AND PRESCRIPTION INSURANCE

Name on Policy: ....

Company: .... Phone: ....

Policy Number: .... Policy Stored Where? ....

Coverage: ....

Notes:...

....

Name on Policy: ....

Company: .... Phone: ....

Policy Number: .... Policy Stored Where? ....

Coverage: ....

Notes:...

....

Name on Policy: ....

Company: .... Phone: ....

Policy Number: .... Policy Stored Where? ....

Coverage: ....

Notes:...

LIFE INSURANCE

Name on Policy: ....

Company: .... Phone Number: ....

Agent: .... Phone Number: ....

Policy Number: .... Policy Stored Where? ....

Amount: .... Whole Life or Term: .... Length of Policy: ....

Notes: ....

Beneficiary Name: .... Phone Number: ....

Beneficiary Address: .... Aware of Designation? ....

Contingent Name: .... Phone Number: ....

Name on Policy: ....

Company: .... Phone Number: ....

Agent: .... Phone Number: ....

Policy Number: .... Policy Stored Where? ....

Amount: .... Whole Life or Term: .... Length of Policy: ....

Notes: ....

Beneficiary Name: .... Phone Number: ....

Beneficiary Address: .... Aware of Designation? ....

Contingent Name: .... Phone Number: ....

Do you have other employee/retiree supplemental life insurance plans? Yes/No
Plan Name: ....

Details: ....

Do you have other employee/retiree supplemental life insurance plans? Yes/No
Plan Name: ....

Details: ....

ADDITIONAL INSURANCE

Type: ....

Company: .... Amount: ....

Policy Number: .... Stored? ....

Agent Name: .... Phone Number: ....

Notes: ....

Type: ....

Company: .... Amount: ....

Policy Number: .... Stored? ....

Agent Name: .... Phone Number: ....

Notes: ....

Type: ....

Company: .... Amount: ....

Policy Number: .... Stored? ....

Agent Name: .... Phone Number: ....

Notes: ....

Type: ....

Company: .... Amount: ....

Policy Number: .... Stored? ....

Agent Name: .... Phone Number: ....

Notes: ....

Type: ....

Company: .... Amount: ....

Policy Number: .... Stored? ....

Agent Name: .... Phone Number: ....

Notes: ....

INCOME TAX FILING

Where do you store copies of previous years? ....

Accountant's Name: ....

Accountant's Phone Number: ....

Accountant's Address: ....

Notes:..

ADDITIONAL FINANCIAL INFORMATION

Notes:..

....

....

....

....

....

....

....

....

....

....

....

....

....

....

....

....

....

....

....

....

ASSETS

REAL ESTATE

Property Type: .... Home, Investment, Rental, Vacation

Address: ....

Purchase Date: .... Payment: ....

Mortgage Held By: ....

Balance of Loan: .... As of date: ....

Value of Property: .... As of date: ....

Homeowners Insurance Company: ....

Property Tax Amount-How are they paid?: ....

Property Type: .... Home, Investment, Rental, Vacation

Address: ....

Purchase Date: .... Payment: ....

Mortgage Held By: ....

Balance of Loan: .... As of date: ....

Value of Property: .... As of date: ....

Homeowners Insurance Company: ....

Property Tax Amount-How are they paid?: ....

Property Type: .... Home, Investment, Rental, Vacation

Address: ....

Purchase Date: .... Payment: ....

Mortgage Held By: ....

Balance of Loan: .... As of date: ....

Value of Property: .... As of date: ....

Homeowners Insurance Company: ....

Property Tax Amount-How are they paid?: ....

STORAGE OF CODES, KEYS AND PROPERTY

Garage Door Code:.............................Secuirty System Code:..................................

Where do you keep extra keys for your house, cars? ....

....

....

Do you have a Storage Unit? Details: ....

....

DOCUMENT AND VALUABLES STORAGE

Do you have a Safe Deposit Box? Y/N   Where is it?   Where is code or key?

....

Do you have a Fireproof Lockbox? Y/N   Where is it?   Where is code or key?

....

STORED ASSETS

Don't let your hidden assets be lost forever. Include information about any secret locations here. Or, write down the details and store them in a safety deposit or lockbox to protect your assets.

Do you have assets hidden in your home?   Y/N Where? ....

Does anyone else know the location? Y/N If yes, who? ....

If no one else knows, you should share the location or an obvious hint.

Location or hint? ....

....

Do you have assets stored in another location?   Y/N Where? ....

Does anyone else know the location? Y/N If yes, who? ....

If no one else knows, you should share the location or give an obvious hint.

Location or hint? ....

....

VEHICLES

Vehicle Type: .... * Automobile, Boat, Motorhome, Motorcycle, Truck

Make: .... Model: .... Year: ....

Registered To: .... VIN#: ....

Status of Ownership: .... Title Stored? ....

Vehicle Type: .... * Automobile, Boat, Motorhome, Motorcycle, Truck

Make: .... Model: .... Year: ....

Registered To: .... VIN#: ....

Status of Ownership: .... Title Stored? ....

Vehicle Type: .... * Automobile, Boat, Motorhome, Motorcycle, Truck

Make: .... Model: .... Year: ....

Registered To: .... VIN#: ....

Status of Ownership: .... Title Stored? ....

Vehicle Type: .... * Automobile, Boat, Motorhome, Motorcycle, Truck

Make: .... Model: .... Year: ....

Registered To: .... VIN#: ....

Status of Ownership: .... Title Stored? ....

Vehicle Type: .... * Automobile, Boat, Motorhome, Motorcycle, Truck

Make: .... Model: .... Year: ....

Registered To: .... VIN#: ....

Status of Ownership: .... Title Stored? ....

LOAN AGREEMENTS - Money you are owed

The following are loans that you have given to other people or companies.

To Whom: .... Amount: ....

Contact Information: ....

What are the details of the loan and where is the Promissory Note?

....

To Whom: .... Amount: ....

Contact Information: ....

What are the details of the loan and where is the Promissory Note?

....

To Whom: .... Amount: ....

Contact Information: ....

What are the details of the loan and where is the Promissory Note?

....

ADDITIONAL INFORMATION ABOUT ASSETS

....

....

....

....

....

....

....

....

....

....

....

PERSONAL PROPERTY

This section covers different categories of items, such as jewelry, coins, firearms, artwork, collectibles, etc. We recommend you have your items appraised and obtain the proper insurance to cover them in case of loss due to theft, flood, fire, or natural disaster.

Category Name: ....

Have you had any of the items appraised?   Y/N

Do you have an insurance rider on any of these items?   Y/N

Have you videotaped or photographed any of these items?   Y/N

Where are the photos and/or videos stored? ....

Notes or list items: ....

....

....

....

....

Category Name: ....

Have you had any of the items appraised?   Y/N

Do you have an insurance rider on any of these items?   Y/N

Have you videotaped or photographed any of these items?   Y/N

Where are the photos and/or videos stored? ....

Notes or list items: ....

....

....

....

....

PERSONAL PROPERTY

Category Name: ....

Have you had any of the items appraised?   Y/N

Do you have an insurance rider on any of these items?   Y/N

Have you videotaped or photographed any of these items?   Y/N

Where are the photos and/or videos stored? ....

Notes or list items: ....

....

....

....

....

....

Use additional pages to list more items.

....

....

....

....

....

....

....

....

....

....

....

....

ESTATE & LEGAL DOCUMENTS
WILL, TRUST, AND POA

My attorney is: .... Phone: ....

WILL

An attorney is an excellent person to advise you on your Will and ensure that you protect your estate from being overtaxed. In addition, your Will should be kept up-to-date to reflect changes in your family and assets.

Attorney who handled the Will: .... Phone: ....
At the law firm of: ....
Last Will is dated: ....
The executor/executrix is: ....
Are they aware they are the executor? ....
Have you discussed the Will with them? ....
Remind your executor to request multiple copies of your death certificate for accessing your accounts.

My Will is stored: .... A copy is stored: ....
Notes:...
....

ESTABLISHING A TRUST

It may be appropriate to seek your attorney's and financial advisor's advice to determine if establishing a trust fund would benefit your situation.

Do you have a trust? ....
Title of the trust: ....
Trustees and contact information: ....

DURABLE FINANCIAL POWER OF ATTORNEY

A power of attorney gives someone else (your "Agent") the authority to act on your behalf, while you are living, if you become unable to make decisions for yourself, even for a short period. On your financial POA, you can specify the areas where you want to give power to someone else. Upon your death, the executor takes over.

Do you have a financial POA? .... Effective when? ....
Name of your Agent? ....
Where is your financial POA stored? ....

LIVING WILL AND HEALTH CARE POWER OF ATTORNEY

A living will and health care power of attorney instruct family members and physicians on what steps you want to take should you become unable to make health care decisions. Copies are typically only accepted if your living will specifies they are. You should distribute copies or originals to your family, physician, and attorney.

LIVING WILL OR MEDICAL DIRECTIVE

Do you have a Living Will Declaration?................. Effective when?... ....

Do you a DNR? ....

To carry out my Living Will, I designate: ....

Have you discussed your wishes with them? ....

The alternate agent is: ....

My Living Will has been given to: ....

A copy is stored: ....

HEALTH CARE POWER OF ATTORNEY

Do you have a Health Care Power of Attorney? ....

Effective when? ....

I designate as my Health Care POA: ....

Have you discussed your wishes with them? ....

The alternate agent is: ....

My Health Care Directive has been given to: ....

A copy is stored: ....

ORGAN DONATION

I do............................ I do not............................ want any of my organs donated.

I want only the following organs donated: ....
....

Notes:...
....

MEDICAL INFORMATION

Name: .... Date ....

Blood Type .... Height .... Weight ....

DOCTORS *(General Practitioner, Dentist, Specialists, Audiology, Internist, Cardiology)*

Doctor: .... Specialty: ....

Phone: ....

Doctor: .... Specialty: ....

Phone: ....

Doctor: .... Specialty: ....

Phone: ....

Doctor: .... Specialty: ....

Phone: ....

* PATIENT PORTAL INFORMATION – add to PASSWORDS

Veterans Administration Facility: .... Phone: ....

....

Dentist: .... Phone: ....

Eye Doctor: .... Phone: ....

MEDICAL EQUIPMENT

Do you use medical equipment? ....

Who is the supplier? ....

Details? ....

....

MEDICAL CONDITIONS

Do you have any medical conditions or hereditary risk factors that require monitoring?

Please give details. ....

....

....

....

....

Do you have any allergies? Please give details.

....

....

VACCINES AND IMMUNIZATIONS - Type and Date Received

....

....

....

....

....

....

....

....

....

....

....

....

....

MEDICATIONS

Name: .... Pharmacy: ....

Drug Allergies: ....

Drug Name	Treatment of	Started Taking	Dosage	How Often is the Drug Taken?	Prescribed by Whom?

FINAL WISHES

DESIGNATIONS

Do you want to designate someone to carry out your wishes for your funeral? Y/N

If yes, who and have you discussed your wishes with them? ....

Do you have money set aside for your funeral? If yes, where? ....

....

What is your choice for the final disposition of your body?

Burial-traditional in-ground: .... Burial-above ground: ....

Burial-green: .... Cremation-traditional: ....

Placement of cremation ashes? ....

....

RELIGIOUS OR MEMORIAL SERVICE

Type of Service: .... Location ....

Officiant Name: .... Phone Number: ....

FUNERAL HOME

Funeral Home Preference: ....

Contact Name: .... Phone Number: ....

Have you purchased a package from the funeral home? Y/N

CEMETERY

Cemetery Name: ....

I have a plot in the name of: .... The deed is stored: ....

I am entitled to military honors: Y/N   I am entitled to Veteran's benefits: Y/N

NOTES: ....

....

....

VIEWING

If there is a casket, would you like a viewing?

....

OBITUARY

Would you like to write your Obituary, or is there something you want to be mentioned in your Obituary? If so, write it on a separate sheet and add it to the end of the book.

SERVICE

Would you like a religious service or a memorial service?

....

Where would you like the service to be held?

....

Please describe the mood or tone of the service you'd like to have.

....

What hymns or music would you like to be played?

....

Which Bible verses, poetry, or readings would you like to have read?

....

Who would you like to speak?

....

Do you have photos or other remembrances that you'd like displayed? Please describe.

....

Would you like to specify a charity in place of flowers?

....

Would you like to give your guests something at the service, such as a program, memorial card, photograph, or bookmark?

....

Please identify specific people, if any, that you want to be sure are invited to your service.

....

....

....

....

....

MILITARY HONORS

If you are entitled to military honors, a flag presentation, and playing "Taps," would you like to have the benefits? ....

GRAVESIDE

Would you like everyone to be invited to the graveside? ....

Have you purchased a headstone? ....

What type of headstone would you like to have, and what would you like engraved on it? ....
....

Would you like to specify a special reading? ....

Is there someone you would like to speak? ....
....

Would you like people to place something on your casket? ....

RECEPTION

Where would you like the reception to be held? ....
....

Who would you like to be invited? ....
....
....

POST-RECEPTION ACTIVITY

Would you like your friends and loved ones to do something together or individually to honor you? Ideas: a memorial scholarship, taking a walk, stories, etc.

....
....

Additional wishes and thoughts:

....
....
....
....
....

PASSWORDS

Name: ....

Company / Site Address	User ID	Password
Cell Phone		
Computer		

PASSWORDS

Name: ....

Company / Site Address	User ID	Password

MONTHLY BILLS

Company: .... Phone number: ....

Account number: .... Contact name: ....

Bill received by mail or email: ....

What address: ....

How do you pay? .... *Check, Website, Auto-Debit

How often do you pay? .... What amount? ....

*Full, Minimum, Other

Company: .... Phone number: ....

Account number: .... Contact name: ....

Bill received by mail or email: ....

What address: ....

How do you pay? .... *Check, Website, Auto-Debit

How often do you pay? .... What amount? ....

*Full, Minimum, Other

Company: .... Phone number: ....

Account number: .... Contact name: ....

Bill received by mail or email: ....

What address: ....

How do you pay? .... *Check, Website, Auto-Debit

How often do you pay? .... What amount? ....

*Full, Minimum, Other

Company: .... Phone number: ....

Account number: .... Contact name: ....

Bill received by mail or email: ....

What address: ....

How do you pay? .... *Check, Website, Auto-Debit

How often do you pay? .... What amount? ....

MONTHLY BILLS

Company: .... Phone number: ....

Account number: .... Contact name: ....

Bill received by mail or email: ....

What address: ....

How do you pay? .... *Check, Website, Auto-Debit

How often do you pay? .... What amount? ....

*Full, Minimum, Other

Company: .... Phone number: ....

Account number: .... Contact name: ,...........................

Bill received by mail or email: ....

What address: ....

How do you pay? .... *Check, Website, Auto-Debit

How often do you pay? .... What amount? ....

*Full, Minimum, Other

Company: .... Phone number: ....

Account number: .... Contact name: ....

Bill received by mail or email: ....

What address: ....

How do you pay? .... *Check, Website, Auto-Debit

How often do you pay? .... What amount? ....

*Full, Minimum, Other

If you have additional monthly bills, write them on a
separate sheet of paper and store them inside this book.

SUBSCRIPTIONS, MEMBERSHIPS, AND PUBLICATIONS

Make a list of all your online and print accounts with dues or payments. You may add log-in information here or on the password page.

....
....
....
....
....
....
....
....
....
....
....
....
....
....
....
....
....
....
....
....
....
....
....
....
....

THOUGHTS, WORDS, AND WISHES

IF I'M UNABLE TO COMMUNICATE,

please take care of the following items:

....

....

....

....

....

....

....

....

....

....

....

....

....

....

....

....

....

....

....

....

....

ADDITIONAL INFORMATION

Include anything that is not covered in any other section.

....

....

....

....

....

....

....

....

....

....

....

....

....

....

....

....

....

....

....

....

....

A FEW MEMORABLE MOMENTS

LETTER TO A LOVED ONE

LETTER TO A LOVED ONE

17947097R00031